D1291353

Butterflies and Moths

by Susan Ring

Table of Contents

Introduction

They swoop and flutter. They fill our lives with bright colors. But how much do you really know about butterflies and moths? There are about 20,000 different kinds of butterflies in the world. And there are more than 250,000 different types of moths.

Butterflies and moths are found on every continent except Antarctica. They live on mountains and in meadows. Some thrive in cold climates. But most butterflies and moths prefer warm places, like rain forests. Both butterflies and moths begin life as tiny eggs that hatch into caterpillars. Rain forests have plants for these caterpillars to eat. There are also a lot of flowers in rain forests. Adult moths and butterflies sip on the sweet nectar of these flowers.

Butterflies and moths play an important role in nature. They take pollen from flower to flower. They are also food for many other creatures, such as lizards, spiders, and birds.

The word *butterfly* comes from this yellow butterfly, called a Brimstone. Years ago people called it a "butter-colored fly."

Chapter 1
Butterflies

Like all insects, butterflies have three body parts. The parts are called the head, the **thorax**, and the **abdomen**. Attached to the head are two **antennae** with round knobs at the end. Antennae help the butterfly sense its surroundings. Butterflies also have six legs and four wings. The wings are made up of tiny scales. Wings are strong but light. Some butterflies can fly as fast as 30 miles per hour (48 km/h).

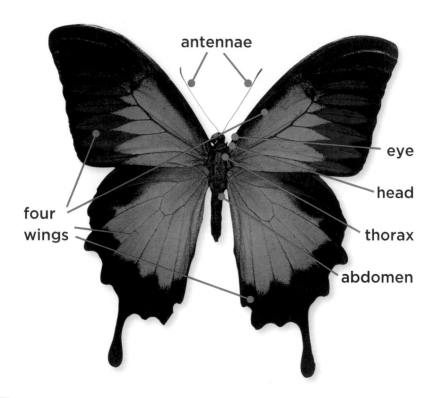

antennae

eye

head

four
wings

thorax

abdomen

⬆ The Queen Alexandra is the largest butterfly in the world. It lives in rain forests in southeast Asia.

Butterflies come in many shapes, sizes, and colors. The largest butterfly in the world has a wingspan that is almost as wide as a 12-inch (30.48 cm) ruler. The smallest butterfly is about the size of a bee. Its wingspan is less than one inch (2.54 cm).

You may know that some birds fly south in the winter. Many butterflies and moths do too, but only one kind of butterfly truly migrates. Monarch butterflies fly south when it gets cold in the north. They return to where they started later in the year. These butterflies can cover 1,000 miles (1,609 km) in a few days. In all, the trip can be more than 4,000 miles (6,437 km) long.

Monarch Migration Routes

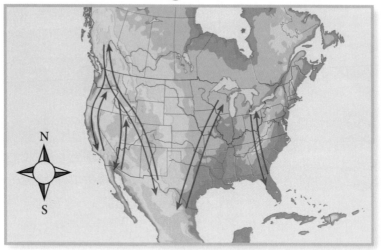

◐ Astronomers and other scientists think that monarchs might use the sun to help them find their way as they migrate.

MONARCH
BUTTERFLY

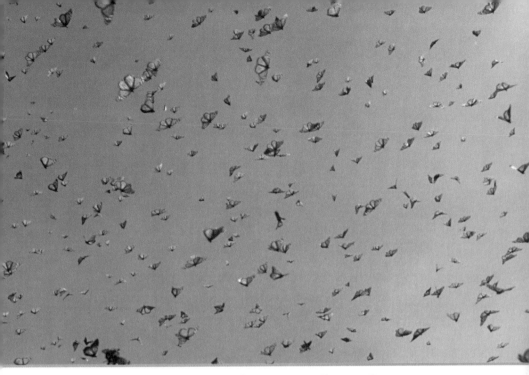

⋂ Some butterflies are solitary. But monarchs travel in large groups.

But that's not the only interesting thing about their journey. Monarch butterfly eggs hatch in the South during the warm winter months. The caterpillars grow into adult butterflies. It is these new monarch butterflies that make the trip back north. These butterflies know exactly where to go and when to fly even though they have never made the trip before. They visit the same territory as the butterflies that went before them.

Chapter 2
Moths

Moths have the same three body parts as butterflies. Some moths have simple straight antennae. Others have antennae that look like feathers.

Some moths eat crops and can destroy a farmers' fruit trees. But most moths help flowers grow. Like butterflies, moths fly from flower to flower, spreading pollen.

◐ This moth investigates its surroundings with its large, feathery antennae.

ROBIN
MOTH

Butterfly or Moth?

Butterflies

- Active during the day

- Rest with wings folded up behind their backs

- Have slim bodies

- Have antennae with round knobs at the ends

Moths

- Active at night

- Rest with wings open flat

- Have fat bodies

- Have straight or feathery antennae

↺ Moths have been on Earth for millions of years. They were flying around the dinosaurs during prehistoric times.

MADAGASCAN
SUNSET MOTH

⏶ Most moths fly at night. These moths are less
colorful than butterflies. But some brightly
colored moths fly during the day.

Most large moths live off food that
was stored in their bodies when they were
caterpillars. This food lasts into their adult lives.

The atlas moth is the ➲
largest moth in the
world. It is the size
of a dinner plate!

Moths that do eat have very long tongues. The tongue stays rolled up under the insect's head. When it is ready to eat, the moth unrolls its tongue and sticks it into a flower. Then, using its tongue like a straw, the moth sips the sweet nectar.

↻ This hummingbird moth is using its long tongue to feed from a milkweed flower.

11

Senses and Defenses

PAINTED LADY
BUTTERFLY

Butterflies and moths have taste buds on their tongues. But female butterflies and moths also taste with their feet. Before she lays her eggs, this butterfly tests the plant with her feet. She makes sure that her young will be able to eat the plant as soon as they hatch.

Moths and butterflies also rely on their sense of smell. But they don't have noses. They pick up different scents with their antennae. A male luna moth can pick up the scent of a female moth from 5 miles (8 km) away!

Birds, monkeys, and lizards all like to eat butterflies and moths. So the insects must find ways to protect themselves. And they do it in some very clever ways.

Camouflage helps some butterflies and moths blend in with their surroundings. Some moths have one color on top of their wings and another color beneath. That way they can blend in with a leaf or a twig.

Color is also used for communication. Bright colors often warn enemies that a butterfly or moth is poisonous or tastes bad.

↶ Some moths have huge eyespots on their wings. The eyespots of the Polyphemus moth look like the eyes of a larger animal.

Chapter 3
Changes

A caterpillar looks nothing at all like an adult butterfly. So how does this change occur? First a female butterfly finds the perfect place to lay her eggs. When each butterfly egg hatches, a tiny **larva** crawls out and immediately starts eating. This larva is called a caterpillar.

1. The caterpillar **molts**.

2. The caterpillar spins a silk knob to attach itself to a stem.

3. The butterfly forms inside the **chrysalis** during the **pupa** stage.

The caterpillar eats until its next stage of life. It doesn't sip nutrients like an adult butterfly does. It has jaws made for munching leaves.

The caterpillar keeps growing. But its skin does not grow at the same rate. The caterpillar must molt—shed its skin—as it grows. The caterpillar molts about six times in all. Before its last molt, it attaches itself to a stem. At this stage the caterpillar is called a pupa. The pupa hangs on without moving. But changes are happening inside. Finally a butterfly appears.

The butterfly breaks through the chrysalis.

5. The butterfly dries its wet, crumpled wings in the air.

6. A few hours later, the butterfly has spread its wings. It is ready to fly.

Moths go through incredible changes too. Like butterflies, female moths lay eggs that hatch as larvae—also called caterpillars—that grow and molt over time.

When a moth caterpillar is ready to become a pupa, it spins a **cocoon**. The cocoon covers the caterpillar while it changes into a moth. Some moth caterpillars make their cocoons underground. Others make them in trees. A cocoon gives good protection. It can even help a pupa overcome cold weather.

↻ Some female moths lay hundreds of eggs. These eggs take about two weeks to hatch.

Some moth cocoons—like this one—blend in with tree bark or dead leaves. Others blend in with green leaves. Either way, camouflage helps the pupa stay safe.

Finally, when the moth is ready, it must force its way out of the cocoon. The cocoon can be very hard. Some moths cut their way out with a special organ on their bodies. Others soften the walls with a special liquid.

Conclusion

For many years people collected butterflies and moths. Today it is against the law to capture many kinds of insects. It is important to protect them from dying out.

One way you can enjoy butterflies and moths is by making a butterfly garden. Butterflies and moths like to visit certain flowers and bushes. You can also have plants where the female insects can lay their eggs. With this garden you will be able to observe these extraordinary insects and help them survive.

Glossary

abdomen *(AB-duh-muhn)* the rear part of an insect's body *(page 4)*

antennae *(an-TEN-ee)* a pair of long, thin feelers that allow an insect to sense its surroundings; the singular is **antenna** *(an-TEN-uh)* *(page 4)*

chrysalis *(KRIS-uh-lis)* the hard outer protection made by a caterpillar that protects it as it changes into a butterfly *(page 14)*

cocoon *(kuh-KEWN)* a silky covering that a caterpillar spins around itself to protect it while it changes into a moth *(page 16)*

larva *(LAHR-vuh)* the newly hatched form of some insects and some animals. A caterpillar is the larva of a moth or butterfly. The plural is **larvae** *(LAHR-vee)*. *(page 14)*

molt *(MOHLT)* to grow out of, or shed, old skin and grow new skin *(page 14)*

pupa *(PYEW-puh)* the development stage during which a caterpillar changes into a butterfly or moth *(page 14)*

thorax *(THAWR-aks)* the middle part of an insect's body *(page 4)*

Index

Comprehension Check

Summarize

Use a Description Chart to list words from this book that describe butterflies and moths. Then use the chart to summarize the information in the book.

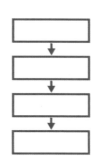

Think and Compare

1. Skim page 13. What are some of the different ways butterflies and moths protect themselves from their enemies? *(Identify Text Structure: Description)*

2. Butterflies and moths rely a great deal on their different senses. Which of your senses do you use the most? Why? *(Apply)*

3. Many butterflies and moths are losing their habitats. If butterflies and moths disappeared altogether, how would it affect the world around us? *(Analyze)*